Most People Dream Of Being Rich But Are

Terrified Of Losing Money

Destiny S. Harris

I0407076

. . .

. . .

1st Free Gift!

Giving Rocks.

I give away free books daily.

Get your free books today.

Here's how

Step 1: Visit amazon.com/author/destinyharris

Step 2: Filter books by "Price: Low to High"

Step 3: Download available free books

. . .

Table of Contents

. . .

Introduction

There are no shortcuts to building wealth.

To make money and build wealth, you have to invest.

That investment could be any of the following:

1. Time
2. **Money**
3. Knowledge

Eventually, you will need to invest money.

If you don't invest your money, it burns and deteriorates due to inflation.

But people don't like investing because when you invest your money, you set yourself up to potentially lose money, and people hate <u>losing</u>.

For most people, the reason they don't win financially is that the pain of losing money is far greater than the joy of being rich (Robert T. Kiyosaki).

Which desire is strongest for you?

- The desire to build wealth.
- The desire to stay safe.

Whichever desire is strongest will create your financial outcomes.

. . .

Emotional Regulation Is Important For Investing

I was always an <u>unemotional investor</u>.

When the losses come, they come.

When the wins come, they come.

I don't necessarily celebrate either way because the balance will increase no matter what happens.

When you invest prudently, the value of your assets increases — whether your investments are winning or losing.

And if your assets are losing, they will bounce back, or there will be another opportunity you can seize to create a better avenue for your money.

Playing It Safe Will Keep You Broke

If you're not investing your money, **you're not winning.**

If you're scared to lose money and desire to build wealth the slow way, great, but understand that means you should start investing when you're 20.

Most start *seriously* investing when they're in their 30s, 40s, 50s, and 60s.

If you're in these age brackets, these are the times when you must take more calculated but prudent risks to help you bridge the gap (and make up for lost time) as much as possible to build wealth.

The only way to take prudent and calculated risks is to study, learn, and acquire knowledge.

The more you learn, the more informed decisions you can make with your money.

The One Thing All Wealthy People Do With Their Money

Wealthy people put their money to work.

They don't let it sit around.

And the more money they put to work, the harder their money works for them.

I recall a professional athlete's financial manager coaxing him to invest more money.

Once he understood how much winnings he could earn from his investments, he was sold and started investing even more than his financial advisor originally proposed.

Wealthy people invest their money by taking calculated risks.

They're comfortable taking risks because of the potential rewards, which are usually always on the other side of risks.

Broke people stay broke because they never take risks.

It's not sexy **NOT** to be an investor.

When I have conversations with 40-year-olds and ask about their financial status, too many say they need to get started or know better than to invest their money, which is why they're broke.

Do you want to be broke, or do you want to be wealthy?

Thank You For Reading

Thank you for reading this book.

Stay blessed, lucky, favored, aware, and joyous.

. . .

The End.

. . .

About Destiny S. Harris

Destiny S. Harris' goal is to positively inspire, cultivate, elevate, and educate the minds of individuals across the globe through her writing.

Creating (whether books, courses, articles, poetry, or music) has always been Destiny's thing, not to mention health & fitness and all things entrepreneurial. Destiny published her first book, "Beauty Secrets for Girls," at age 11 and her second book, "Don't Wait Until It's Too Late," at age 12.

Destiny obtained three degrees from the University of Georgia in Psychology, Political

Science, & Cultural Studies. She also started her own music teaching business at the age of 14, which she led for over ten years. In addition, she has been teaching academic, career, and personal development topics to thousands of students and readers since 2004.

Outside of writing, Destiny loves and enjoys a few other things: reading, bodybuilding, traveling, dogs, food, classic movies, anime, mountain and ocean views, plants, and nature.

Check out her work, leave a review, share your thoughts with your friends and family, and be a part of a movement: helping people learn and grow through means of self-education (books).

Complete the Steps To Get Free eBooks:

Step 1: Go to amazon.com/author/destinyharris

Step 2: Filter books by "Price: Low to High"

Step 3: Download available free books

. . .

Connect W/ Destiny S. Harris

Please reach out and stay in touch. Destiny S.

Harris enjoys chatting with readers.

Start a conversation today @ destinyh.com

. . .

Free Gifts!

Access courses & books at the link below:

destinyh.com

. . .